ORPHAN POEMS

by Jenni Finlay

Illustrations by Emily Richter

Cover Design by Marc Harkness
and Emily Richter

FIRST EDITION, 2016
Copyright © 2016 by Jenni Finlay
All Rights Reserved
ISBN-13: 978-0-9837383-8-1

Library of Congress Control Number: 2016912025

No part of this book may be performed,
recorded, thieved, or otherwise transmitted
without the written consent of the author and
the permission of the publisher. However,
portions of poems may be cited for book
reviews—favorable or otherwise—without
obtaining consent.

MEZCALITA PRESS, LLC
Norman, Oklahoma

ORPHAN POEMS

by Jenni Finlay

For all the collective orphans
who have been left a little emptier
since Kent Finlay left the earth.

TABLE OF CONTENTS

Acknowledgements x
Foreword xii
Introduction xiv

Latest Song 3
And then you die 7
The Morning After 9
Never Again 11
HalleyAnna 12
The Hill Country Choir 14
You really like messing with me,
    don'cha 17
Monarch Migration 19
Saturday Mourning 21
Chess 22
You made me smile through
    my tears 23
Strange Hotel Room 25
Later that night
    I go downstairs 26
We left a little
    at Luckenbach 28

"Well, it looks like I haven't been here
    in a while" 31
Chicken one day,
    feathers the next 32
Flood A'Coming 33
Sterling got sick 35
And then Victor died 36
The Kid 38
Thanksgiving 40
Spaghetti 43
Sleep in Heavenly Peace 44
Christmas Day 47
It's Sunday,
    so I thought I'd call 49
New Year 51
Sterling died twice 52
Happy Birthday 54
March 2, 2016 56

Bios 62

"Tomorrow's all today is all about."

~ Kent Finlay, *The Songwriter*

Illustrations by:

Emily Richter

Cover Illustration by:

Marc Harkness and Emily Richter

Based on photo by:

Brian T. Atkinson

Edited by:

Brian T. Atkinson
Ashley Stanberry Brown

ACKNOWLEDGEMENTS

Special thanks to Nathan and Ashley Brown and Mezcalita Press for believing once again that words could flow through my pen.

Thanks to James McMurtry, Kellie Salome, Curtis McMurtry, Robert Kraft, Jon Dee Graham, Gretchen and William Harries Graham for helping me through the fog of the first few hours, days and months.

Thanks to Mary Bruton, Walt Wilkins, Marc Harkness, Mandy Brown, Kara Remme and Dave Insley, Super Dave, Eric and Debbie Beverly, The Lambert Family, Tamara Saviano, Joan Kornblith, Lou and Raine DeMarco, Rod Picott, Adam and Chris Carroll, Owen Temple, Brennen Leigh and Noel McKay, Beth Lavinder, Russell Tanner, Troy Campbell, Alan Lazarus and Enoteca, who sustained me throughout.

Thanks to the Hill Country Choir and Cheatham Street Warehouse.

Thanks to The Arlington Hotel and Jim Coleman Crystal Mines in Hot Springs, Arkansas for their hospitality as I wrote the bulk of this book.

Thanks to my family for living through it with me.

Very special thanks to Clay, who thinks I can do anything, and Brian who always calls me on my bullshit.

Mostly, thanks to Dad, for listening to me rattle on even still.

FOREWORD

This collection of poems you hold in your hand has had quite a hold on me for a while now. These are the work of Jenni Finlay, as she recollects, grieves and works through the loss of her father, best friend and soulmate – Kent Finlay, the songwriter, performer, mentor, raconteur and Texas treasure.

These are true works of art, full of the elements that make life…well, life. Sorrow, work, sickness, friends, family, humor, moments of transcendence and death. They are unflinching as they look evenly, broken-heartedly and gratefully at life's hardest chapter: losing someone closest to you.

These poems are personal, yes, and universal and conversational. I guarantee you some tears. Good tears. But also some real smiles and even good laughs.

There is a line in here that is one for the ages; I've laughed out loud, by myself, every time I've read it. Every poem is meaningful. The preface of the collection, the Eulogy, is a masterpiece.

Thank you, Jenni, my friend and fellow traveler, for getting this done. It's wonderful, a testament to many things I hold most dear. Like so many of us, I am grateful for Kent's life and friendship and I am grateful for you sharing these pictures of the toughest year of your life. I can see the "pride all over his face" right now.

~ Walt Wilkins,
sitting by the Colorado River
on April 26, 2016 at 6:22 am

INTRODUCTION

The Eulogy

We've been wiggling through Texas all week and are finally heading back home from some fairground's flatbed trailer stage. My hair still smells like funnel cakes and cotton candy.

Dad chooses a back road that winds through his old stomping ground, Fife, Texas, the place he feels most at home. We stop at the Finlay family cemetery and wander through our generations: Finlays, Shorts, Mitchells.

I walk around aimlessly for a while and then look back. Dad's stopped. He's staring at his father's headstone. His head nods softly toward the ground.

I think about the first time my dad described the grandfather I was too young to meet, James Finlay, Jr.: "He was the strongest man that ever lived," Dad said. "Daddy was strong in every way. He did things well. He could shoot a jackrabbit in the head at two hundred yards with a twenty-two."

My father stands at his father's headstone. Seconds turn into minutes as he shakes his head over and over. Then suddenly, he looks up and signals toward our old orange Chevy van.

We walk over together, climb in and start the five-hour trip home. We don't speak. I tuck my legs under myself and curl up in the overstuffed front-seat captain's chair, resting my head against the threadbare arm.

My father weeps gently. I listen to the air and gravel out the window and cautiously eye him. He coughs and tries to shake it off, noticing that I'm watching him.

I'm nine years old, unsure and uncomfortable. So I sing: "Talking to myself again, wondering if this traveling is good…" Dad loves singing in the van. We learned this John Sebastian song off an Everly Brothers cassette and it's one of his favorites. It's not one of mine. I know we're not working this one up for a gig and we don't have time to sing "for fun." We have plenty to learn for work already.

Dad's still softly choking back tears, though, so I have to do something. This is what I do. It's the only way I know to say, "It'll be okay, Dad."

"Is there something better you and I'd be doing if we could…" I wait while Dad stares straight ahead. I can't read him like usual – my friend, father and duo partner. I realize I'm holding my breath unintentionally, but I can't let myself breathe just yet. Then he sings:

"But oh the stories we could tell and if this all blows up and goes to hell." I sing harmony and Dad's tears turn into a smile. "I can still see us sitting on a bed in some motel singing all the stories we could tell."

We sing the song together and we sing another and another, all the way home. Our harmonies fill the air the entire trip.

"Thank you for that," Dad says hours later when we climb out of the van and unload the gear. "Thank you."

I stand here today at my father's memorial. But suddenly I'm whisked back in time. I can see Dad there bird-doggin' our old van right now. And all I want to do is walk over to him and climb in and head back to the house.

But of course, I can't. He's left without me. I'm no longer nine, but I'm still unsure and uncomfortable.
Sad. Lonely.
Really, really lonely without my dad.

But you know what? I also feel incredibly blessed.

Grateful. Thankful.

Think about what a man he was! Sitting in the captain's chair by Dad's side, I learned so many lessons in integrity and inspiration. Dedication and devotion.

Living life to the fullest. Dreaming.
Making dreams come true.

I can tell you without a doubt:

He was the strongest man
that ever lived.

ORPHAN POEMS

Latest Song

You call for help organizing
your latest song.
The clock reads ten o'clock at night.
I tell you I'll call you right back.
I throw my heaviest coat
over my PJs
and race to Brian's house
where the tape recorder
is hooked to the landline.

When I call you
the recorder's running
and I have no idea what to expect.

"Okay," I say.
"Okay," you repeat back.

And you begin
to tell me the bad news
the only way you can,
through your new song.

Your words immediately
still my breathing:
"The last thing I want to do is die."

"Verse one goes like this," you say,
"and here's the chorus
and then here's verse two.
I need two more lines here."
You catch your breath as I wait.

*"Life is an hour glass
and I'm a grain of sand
Somebody hold my hand."*

I'm speechless after
you sing the last line.
"Did you get all that?" you ask directly.
Silence holds the air for three beats.
"Yeah," I croak softly.

"You need me to repeat any of it?
Is it all there?"

"Well," I say – stalling, sobbing,
"maybe you need a bridge."

You laugh gently.
Of course you know what I'm doing.
"What would it say?"

"I don't know," I choke past the tears.
"It may take a long time to figure out."

And then you die

The Morning After

My oldest friend, my highest hero,
my everything under the sun.
No more.
The world mourns all around me
yet leaves me all alone.
All of a sudden, I don't remember
how to fall asleep or wake up
or fill the coffee cup.
All I feel is the spinning sadness.

I never really told you
you were my biggest supporter,
my closest confidant,
the one person in the world
who thought I could do no wrong.
You were everything
that made me Jenni Finlay.
No longer can I pick up the phone
or sit across plates of enchiladas
and hear that enthusiastic
"Well, all right! Mighty fine!
You done good!"

I'm not gonna lie:
I'm totally lost.
Alone.
Heartless.
Wingless.
No way home.
No way out.

My lifeless body crawls from the bed
the next morning,
numb and stunned.
Friends are over,
some I expected and some I didn't.
Even James shows up.
"Man, you know you're in bad shape,"
Brian says, "when James McMurtry
comes over to cheer you up."
Then it hits me:
People will take care of my heart,
friends will lift me up.
The very best will cover me
from the storm.

Never Again

Never again will I have someone
who remembers
our past
our stories
inside jokes
our favorite punch lines:

BUZZARD VOMIT!!!
...

...

...See?

HalleyAnna

HalleyAnna doesn't want to record.
I get it.
I don't either,
but we have a session booked
the day after your death
for your tribute record.

I push her to do it,
my stubbornness matching hers.
HalleyAnna furrows her eyebrows,
bites the side of her cheek,
sips her Lone Star
and shakes off her doubts.

All fussy and determined,
she steps confidently into the booth.
Damn!
My little sister nails it!
She sings your epitaph with more
raw emotion than I've ever seen.
"I've written some life," the words go,
"I've lived some songs."

She doesn't shed a tear,
but we all weep silently,

watching her blossom from a plucky kid
into mature woman,
shattered and somber and doing her best
to move forward.

The Hill Country Choir

We didn't think we were even going to
include your greatest hit
on this tribute album
but then again
you were never supposed to die.

Jamie Lin Wilson cuts "Hill Country"
in one take and changes
the whole record.
We immediately scrap everything
we had: the previously recorded songs,
live tracks and rough cuts,
the whole hodgepodge.
Now the whole world's different.
We start from the beginning.

Now, this record's a true tribute,
a salute to the life you led
by the songwriters you inspired
recording your songs,
those rhymes and rhythms,
the wisdom of your words
so few heard during your lifetime.

Droves numbly gather at the studio
the next night and form
the Hill Country Choir,
hundreds of songwriters
that you influenced
singing the last two choruses
of your best loved song.

Holding onto each other
we sing arm in arm,
broken hearts bursting open.
"They call it the Hill Country,
I call it beautiful."

Wiping away tears, we look to the sky,
singing and swaying
through our own grief and sadness,
singing for you before
filing out gradually
heads hung low
into the dark.

To this day, I hear your voice
mingled with the mourning choir
belting out the last chorus.

You really like messing with me, don'cha

You do it on purpose, I know.

I straighten the picture frame
and as soon as I turn around
it's crooked again.

You probably get such a chuckle
moving things around just a smidge,
knowing it drives me crazy,
knowing I can't help
but put things back
how they should be.

Monarch Migration

I will watch for the monarchs
as they migrate through Texas this year
like snowbirds from Yankeeland
because I know
if you had your druthers
you'd come back as one of them,
a fierce and fiery flash of color
just to finally figure out
how they always managed to know
the way to go
without little butterfly maps,
unfolded like wings.

Saturday Mourning

You always said before the show:
"We have to get our heads into the gig."
We'd kick off the thirty-minute set
with "Boil Them Cabbage Down"
and close with "Happy Trails."
Red Ropers digging into my ankles,
chinrest digging into my neck,
I'd think to myself:
Remember to smile
and turn on the charm.
Remember the words
to "Long Black Veil."
Today, I mindlessly eat artichokes
for breakfast and peel away
at the leaves,
the morning of the family memorial.
Get your head into the gig, I tell myself.
Get your head into the gig
for the last Kent and Jenni Finlay show.

Chess

The chess board looks a wreck
even a month later.
Pieces picking up the pieces,
the game plays out like this:
The queen bolts to the other side
of the board as soon as
the shit hits the fan.
("Self preservation," she says.)
The bishop artfully angles his way
into the king's old spot.
The rook scooches only
to the very edge of her square
unsure of her next move.
"The king is dead!
Long live the king!" they cry.
The pawns plan
memorial after memorial,
an endless stream of memorials.
The cards have left the knight
to sort everything out,
a kingdom left in a stalemate.

You made me smile through my tears

Alone in my sorrow, I plan a private
memorial – just me,
my thoughts and our memories.
I have it all planned out.
I've bought the candles and incense
after digging for quartz
and crystals all day.
I find a spot surrounded
by Arkansas pines,
red dirt embedded
under my fingernails,
caked on the knees of my jeans.
I set up and sit
and watch the smoke from
the incense trail into the forest.
My tears well up
and my heart drops again.
I lower my head
and feel them running down.
When I look up: smoke rings!
I watch, amazed, and hold my breath
as stick figure after stick figure
emerges from the incense.

No one will believe me –
so I take a picture
as smoky ghosts
I'm sure you have created
in a wispy chorus line
to make me smile
dance their jigs
before fading off into the dusk.

Strange Hotel Room

I wake up this morning
in the wee hours,
the time between wine and coffee,
and finally *feel* again.

Gone is the glorious numbness
that blanketed me
throughout the past two months
from grief and gloom
death and darkness.

Later that night I go downstairs

In my pantyhose and earrings.

I want to commemorate my spiritual
journey, congratulate myself
for not staying safe in my shell.

After a long day of digging for crystals,
the piano man begins playing "Misty"
as I walk into the empty restaurant.
He follows with a rousing medley of
"Amazing Grace" and "Last Date."
I forget to order when he begins
"I Come to the Garden Alone."

I leave my seat tentatively and request
"Don't Let the Stars Get in Your Eyes."
He begins barrelhouse style
just like you would,
slamming down the keys hard,
pedals squeaking under the strain.

The song ends and I start
toward my table.

I pause and turn back.
I only have a ten,
but it fills his wine glass tip jar.
Then I silently toast to you.

We left a little at Luckenbach

I bring some of your ashes
to Luckenbach
after the probate judge
deems your will good and valid.

(He has a band, by the way.
Of course he does.
Played for free on Sundays
when you'd let them.
He asked if there was
an opening right now
and gave me his card
as I stood in front of him in court.)

I put you secretly under that tree
where Darrell broke his Ventura
headstock, the guitar he thought
had no more songs in it,
but you wrote "Written Some Life"
on it anyway.

To spite him, I suppose.

I buy a Pearl beer and cover you
with half and give the rest to Hondo
at his memorial statue
just a few feet away,
your best friend,
your true soul mate.

I imagine the two of you laughing
in the shade,
sharing a beer,
together again.

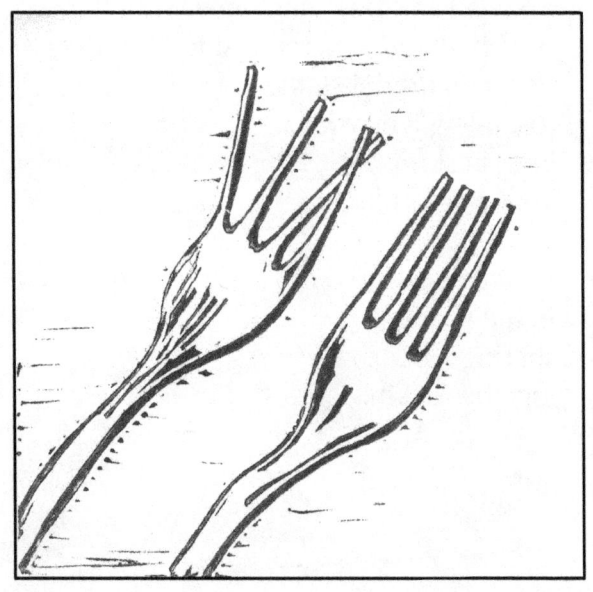

"Well, it looks like I haven't been here in a while"

You would say as you fiddled
with your butter knife at the table.
You always managed to get the one
set of silverware with the screwed up
fork, prongs all uneven and askew.

You'd stare at it sideways,
one eye closed,
as if you were taking target practice.
Then you'd align it and straighten
the prongs with the knife,
weaving in and out ever so carefully.

I'd never had this happen to me,
so I pretty much thought you made it up,
just a fun restaurant trick
as we waited for enchiladas.

And now I think time and time again:
Well, it looks like Dad
hasn't been here in a while…

Chicken one day, feathers the next

We gather family at the house
for a Memorial Day barbeque
and for the first time in a long time
we feel the closeness we had,
all of us together and laughing
and just enjoying one another,
thinking about brighter days ahead.

Later that night rain comes down
and pushes the river up
against our childhood home,
like waves against a ship,
washing all yesterday's innocence away,
leaving us wasted and worried
about tomorrow.

Flood A'Coming

Of course we get the instruments –
including your favorite old Martin
and my first guitar, Old Friend.
We grab the computer and the amps,
the library table your great-grandfather
made by hand with the secret
letter underneath
and the coffee table travel-trunk
your great great grandmother
brought all the way from Scotland, all
the treasures almost wiped from history.

We know all the stories,
but don't tell them; there's no time.
We even get the damn "closette"
you built for me.
(No one thought we'd ever get it
out of the house.)

Hurry, hurry, hurry…
we rescue everything we can,
even the five-hundred-pound antique
barber chair.

You should've seen it
sliding across the river,
heavy grey silt on the tall porches
and driveway. We get it all,
all of your songs as promised.
I grab your favorite wine cup,
the one with the chip in it,
as I walk out the door for (maybe) the
last time. We skid down the driveway
in the rented U-Haul
just as the rain starts again.

Sterling got sick

He stares at me from the hospital bed,
so old and yet so much younger
than I've ever seen him.
His hopeful eight-year-old eyes
look wearily out from behind
a sallowed sixty-year-old face,
afraid and alone,
tattered and torn,
looking for another answer,
a way out.
His heart is broken
from deaths and floods
and self-sabotage.
My little brother,
The Great Persuader,
cannot get out of this one.

And then Victor died

Well, you got yourself a soundman.
Isn't it just like him to get there early
in his cool and nonchalant way,
wondering if he could help set up –
not scheduled, of course, until way later,
but that's just the way he was.

You got yourself a soundman
to amp up the Heavenly Choir
(or whoever you have
playing happy hour)
and fix the mix of the Angel Band.
Hell, he'll even make the posters
to promote the show.

You got yourself a soundman,
a damn good friend,
who I know would rather
still be here with us
picking and playing,
working and writing.

You got yourself a soundman
who can fill in if you need him
for a song-swap in a pinch,
whose song
– with words as strong as warriors –
will inspire Michael
the archangel himself.

Knowing you,
you will want to tweak it just a hair
but won't.

There's no need now.

The Kid

I watch her set her face
in that familiar, determined way,
mouth in a straight line,
eyes dead ahead.

She absently blows a strand
of dark hair away.
The only one you ever
really treated like a kid
is trying to wrap her head
around a world without you.

There was a time you'd listen and laugh
and imagine away her frustrations.
You protected her in every way possible
from most every risk she could ever risk.

Hell, she was never even
in the family band!

The rest of us were seriously jealous –
we were just bandmates
and business partners,

but she was the spunky kid
in your sparkling eyes,
and you'd just grin
and shake your head.

Oh, and she hated it, too.
I suppose that's why
she divorced you.

Thanksgiving

We go to the homestead
smelling of antiques and old memories
for Thanksgiving with the aunts
and uncles and cousins by the dozens.

We talk about the weather
and the cotton crop this year
and high school football
and how everybody's doing.

Aunt Barbara leads the prayer
before the meal.
It's all the same,
as normal as possible,
and so very different.

I'm alone.

Surrounded by family and friends,
I feel incredibly lonesome without you.
Without you bragging about how good
the dressing was this year.
Without you insisting that

you didn't even miss the gravy
Barbara had forgotten to make.
Without you figuring out when *exactly*
the kitchen was first remodeled.

I leave before the music starts.
I don't think I could've stood it.

But I wonder now
who stepped up to take
all the good verses on
"Will The Circle Be Unbroken."

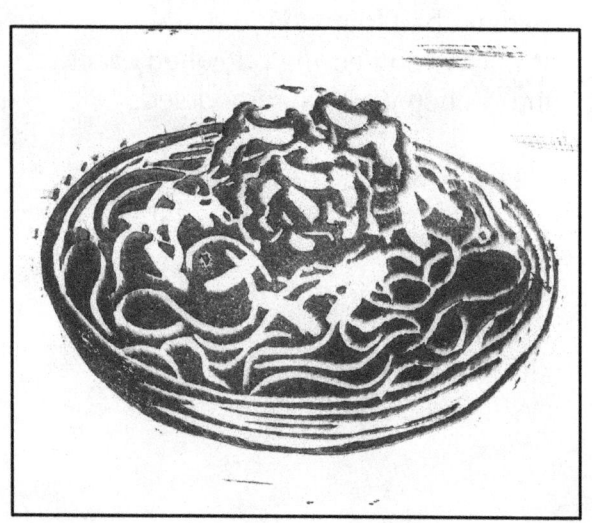

Spaghetti

We pick up the tubs
of to-go spaghetti and recall
sitting with you at Fazoli's,
the aroma of overcooked tomato
and garlic in the air,
hopelessly attempting to keep
the slippery sauce-coated noodles
on our plastic forks, the first thing
you could finally taste again
after treatment took your taste buds.
You said "There once was a time
when I would say, 'Aww, spaghetti,'
but now I say, 'WOW! SPAGHETTI!'"

Sleep in Heavenly Peace

You'd put fruits and veggies
in our Christmas stockings each year.
Most years, I'd get a sweet potato.
Sterling would get a purple onion
(if he was lucky).
HalleyAnna always got a bag of prunes.
It was a big joke every year:
Prunes.

If anyone ever asked, you would say
all you wanted for Christmas was peace.

One year when we were at our highest
bickering point, you announced
that all you wanted was
"Peace in the Family."

Smartasses that we are,
we bought a cheap bottle of Peace brand
chardonnay and all drank it
Christmas morning.

Peace in the Family.
There. Ha.

Goddammit all to hell, Dad.
You finally got what you wanted
this year: Peace. And maybe
a sweet potato in your stocking –
or an onion (if you're lucky).

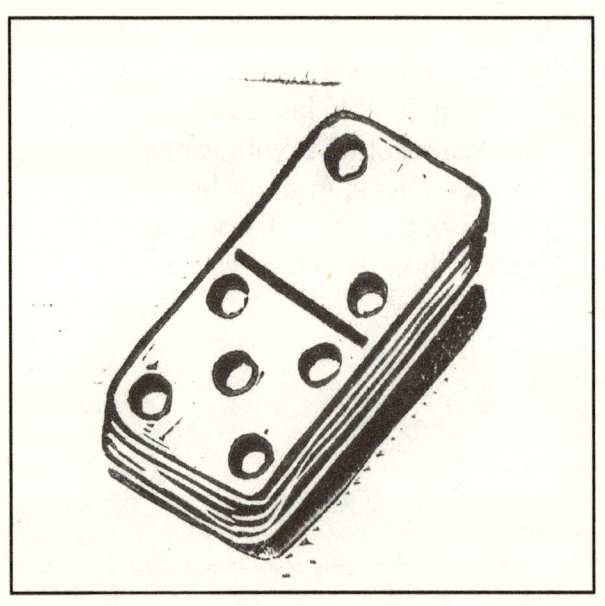

Christmas Day

Cleaning up the kitchen, I overhear
the start of a Mexican Dominoes game:
"Someone shuffle the bones,"
"double-six starts the game."

I look across the remains
of Christmas morning,
wrapping paper crumpled
in corners, small piles of
extra thoughtful gifts,
men comatose by the game and grub.

"You can't play there. Stay in the train."
Slap...Slap...Slap.
I listen to the unmistakable
sound of the dominoes.

It's been a strange day.
We all pulled together – and apart –
and did the best we could.

We didn't realize how hard it could be
to act normal.

It feels like we're starting over again
and we feel your absence more than
ever today.

My hands look old –
pruned and wrinkled
from the dishwater.
"Looks like we all have to go back
to the boneyard,"
I hear her say.
Looks like, I whisper.

It's Sunday so I thought I'd call

Like always.

Back when calls were free on Sunday,
it made sense
calling me up when I was at college.
It became a habit that went beyond
flip-phones or minutes.

"I don't really have any news,"
you'd say.
"Except I finished that song
with Randy Rogers."

Well, I don't have any news today –
except maybe I do.
I got my author's copy
of *Kent Finlay, Dreamer*
and you would've been proud,
so proud to simply hold the book
in your hands, your life story
hard-covered and bound.

It's quiet around here.

I wish I knew if you saw a deer
swim effortlessly across the river
or had an unusually colored bird –
bright blue and neon green –
at your cardinal feeder.

I wish I knew if you found a new
hybrid fruit at the grocery store,
so juicy it ran down your elbows
at the kitchen sink.
Or if your peach tree
is coming back to life
with little buds and bees
and the hope of a good crop.

It's Sunday,
but the phone won't ring.

New Year

You were always serious about
your lucky black-eyed peas
for New Year's.
I can't remember a time in my whole life
when we didn't have them.

If ever anyone complained about
what a crummy year they'd had
and all the bad luck they had to endure,
telling you maybe the peas didn't work
this time, you always said
with a devilish wink,

"Well think about how much worse
it would have been
if you *hadn't* had your black-eyed peas!
Better eat double this year!"

Sterling died twice

They need to test his defibrillator.
Thank goodness Sterling has
always been good at tests.

They kill him for two full minutes
before trying to bring him back.

It doesn't work.

Minutes pass like lifetimes
as they work frantically.
Then finally
he takes his second first breath.

They make minor adjustments,
try again.

Jesus Christ.
Jesus.
Christ.

They kill him again – fingers crossed –
as they wait for the device to kick on.

It works.

Now he takes his third first breath,
all pale skin and messy hair and ribs
poking out, sullen and sickly
and suddenly alive again.
Alive!

Damn, man, what did you guys talk
about? What did you say to Sterling?

You had a full five minutes together!
Did you tell him about the new song
you were working on?
Did you tell him where you left
that dusty boot box full of tax receipts?
Maybe you just stood and looked
at each other.

God, what I would give.

Happy Birthday

I hesitate, but go to the big party,
your annual 29th birthday
anniversary celebration.

Songwriters gather for
the two-day shindig.
One more memorial,
one more wave of grief.

The party doesn't seem the same.
I walk in, stand by your stool
at the end of the bar,
look slowly around.

No one is there to welcome me
like you used to do.
No one is shushing the loud talkers
or running off the drunks.
No one is listening.

When the song is loud,
they only talk louder.
When the song gets soft,

they talk that much softer,
always just a little above
what the night is about.

The marquee light is out.
I walk out into a night,
a little darker than before.

March 2, 2016

You died exactly one year ago.

I just replaced the wreath
that's hung like a dark cloud
on my front door
for three hundred sixty-six days straight,
dust and cobwebs all over the black
bandana I had tied around it.
But I'm not any less sad.
I still have to remind myself every day –
one foot in front of the other,

one foot in front of the other.

It's been such a hard year,
but you know what else?
I started a record label
and co-produced three records
and finished the book about you.
All last year!
Can you believe it?

I can see the pride all over
your face right now,
knowing how far I've come.

I remember reading the manuscript
to you over the phone,
tears spilling out, voice unsteady,
and tripping over my words
while you interrupted
with joyous outbursts:
"Well, all right!"
"Isn't that something?"
"How nice of him to say!"

You were oblivious to my inevitable
sorrow, the salty taste of my tears.

I'd finish every chapter
voice hoarse with emotion,
beat down and worn out.

It's been a year now
and I'm no less sad,
but I can let myself breathe again,
see clearly again, be happy.

Yeah, that's right.
Finally.

I can be happy again.

ORPHAN POEMS

AUTHOR

Jenni Finlay is the author of the poetry collection *Table for One* (Mezcalita Press, 2015). Additionally, Finlay co-authored *Kent Finlay, Dreamer* (Texas A&M University Press, 2016) and served as contributing writer for *Pickers and Poets: The Ruthlessly Poetic Singer-Songwriters of Texas* (Texas A&M University Press, 2016). She co-owns Eight 30 Records and co-produced *Cold and Bitter Tears: The Songs of Ted Hawkins*, Danny Barnes' *Got Myself Together* (Ten Years Later) and *Kent Finlay, Dreamer*. Her Jenni Finlay Promotions business has shaped careers for several dozen iconic Americana music singer-songwriters for the past decade. Finlay presents the monthly series Catfish Concerts, which will release *Catfish Concerts Cookbook: Celebrating Americana's Finest Recipes* (Mezcalita Press, 2017).

ILLUSTRATORS

Emily K. Richter is an Asheville, NC-based artist and designer, and a proud new mother. A graduate of East Carolina University's interior design program, Emily also loves cycling, running, swimming and kayaking in her beloved North Carolina mountains. Her T-shirt art featuring an outdoorsy, banjo-playing Sasquatch has wound up in places as far away as Australia.

Marc Harkness is a designer, illustrator, and musician currently residing in Asheville, North Carolina. Born and raised in the Republic of Panama, Marc has designed packing and posters for Billy Joe Shaver, James McMurtry, the Steep Canyon Rangers, Sarah Lee Guthrie and Johnny Irion, among others. When not at work, he is at play, running and kayaking in the Blue Ridge Mountains.

www.ingramcontent.com/pod-product-compliance
Lightning Source LLC
Chambersburg PA
CBHW051711040426
42446CB00008B/830